SINNERS, JESUS WILL RECEIVE

THE EFFECTS OF TOTAL DEPRAVITY AND LIMITED ATONEMENT ON BIBLICAL EVANGELISM AND MISSIONS

WILLIAM PAYNE

SINNERS, JESUS WILL RECEIVE

WILLIAM PAYNE

NEWC OVENANT
MEDIA

5317 Wye Creek Dr, Frederick, MD 21703-6938
Website: newcovenantmedia.com
Email: info@newcovenantmedia.com
Phone: 301-473-8781 or 800-376-4146
Fax: 240-206-0373

SINNERS, JESUS WILL RECEIVE

THE EFFECTS OF TOTAL DEPRAVITY AND LIMITED ATONEMENT ON BIBLICAL EVANGELISM AND MISSIONS

Published by: New Covenant Media
5317 Wye Creek Drive
Frederick, Maryland 21703-6938

Orders: www.newcovenantmedia.com

Printed in the United States of America

ISBN 13: 978-1-928965-31-2

Scripture quotations are from The Holy Bible, King James Version.

FOREWORD

According to the way hyper-Calvinists think about such things today, Jesus must have made a mistake when he explained so much of the gospel to Nicodemus, as recorded in John 3. Jesus told Nicodemus, "Unless a man is born again, he cannot see the kingdom of God" (v. 3). And later, "Unless a man is born of water and the Spirit, he cannot enter the kingdom of God" (v. 5). Nicodemus was not born again. So according to the way these persons think, Jesus should have stopped the discussion right there. "Come back later when you are born again," he should have said.

In spite of Nicodemus' inability as a spiritually dead man, Jesus actually went on to explain a great deal of the gospel to him. As I look through the first half of the chapter I see Jesus unfolding at least nine important teachings, presumably over a period of many hours on that far off eastern night. He taught Nicodemus about: 1) the need for regeneration (v. 3), 2) the role of the Holy Spirit in regeneration (v. 5-8), 3) the nature of divine revelation (vv. 10-12), 4) the fact of his incarnation (v. 13), 5) the nature and meaning of the atonement (vv. 14, 15), 6) the love of God for sinners (v. 16), 7) judgment (vv. 17-19), 8) the reason for unbelief (v. 20) and 9) the beginning point and nature of the Christian life (v. 21).

What is happening here? Has Jesus forgotten his own teaching about the prior need for the new birth? Is he contradicting himself?

The answer is none of these things. Jesus knew precisely what he was doing, and the reason he proceeded to teach the unregenerate Nicodemus about these important aspects of biblical theology is that he knew that it is through such teaching and not apart from it, that God actually regenerates the individual. It is through the actual preaching and teaching of the word that God saves persons.

Pastor Bill Payne of Canada knows this and wishes all other Calvinists knew it too, which is why he has written this small booklet. Particularly, it grieves him that so many use good theology to undercut the responsibility we have as Christians to do the equally good work of inviting sinners to come to Jesus Christ. True, this is sometimes done wrongly or on the basis of an aberrant theology. We dare not imply that the sinner has the ability in himself to repent of his sin and trust Christ. Regeneration is prior, and it is God's work. But while it is wrong to imply a natural ability on the sinner's part, it is equally wrong to forget that the sinful person must nevertheless repent of sin and have faith in Jesus to save him.

And what about limited (or definite) atonement? There are many, some Calvinists included, who believe that the death of Jesus Christ for his elect only, and not for all persons, necessarily restricts or undercuts evangelism. But it does nothing of the sort. In fact, quite the opposite is the case. The conduct of Jesus is the best and most instructive example. Jesus made clear in his great high priestly prayer, recorded in John 17, that he was neither dying for nor praying for the whole world but rather for his own, whom the Father had given him out of the world. But shortly after this, after he had died and been raised again, he told his disciples that they were to preach the gospel to all people through the whole world, beginning in Jerusalem (Acts 1:7, 8).

It is only because we have a true atonement, as opposed to something that only makes atonement possible, that we have a true gospel to preach.

How so? If you do not understand how this is so, I encourage you to pursue Pastor Payne's booklet. You will find it helpful, and not just in this area. I am convinced that you will understand the gospel better and perceive more clearly the kind of evangelistic preaching we so desperately need in our time if we are to see a strong movement of the Spirit of God and perhaps even the new awakening and revival in North America for which so many of us pray.

James Montgomery Boice, Philadelphia

PART ONE: INVITING SINNERS TO CHRIST

It is a fact for which we ought to be deeply grateful, that we are living in a day when interest in Reformed theology is being revived. This revival of interest has produced a re-examination of various areas of Christian activity, and evangelistic preaching is an area which has received much attention. Within the framework of evangelistic preaching the question of inviting sinners to Christ is of great importance.

I. Inviting Sinners to Christ is Consistent with Reformed Theology

A. The Opposition of Those Questioning Its Legitimacy

Historically there have been those who have denied that sinners should be indiscriminately invited to come to Jesus Christ. It is important to realize that in our own day some take this same position, and we must recognize the danger that a revival of Reformed theology might result in others adopting what I believe is an erroneous and most unfortunate position. Those who believe in this way contend that while the gospel is to be preached and announced in the presence of unconverted people, those unconverted people are not to be directed and exhorted to repent of their sins and believe on the Lord Jesus Christ. Such specific direction and exhortation may be appropriate for those who are 'awakened' and conscious of their need of Christ, but to the careless, indifferent and unbelieving sinners no such exhortation must be given.

One of the reasons given for this position is that 'such invitations are dishonoring to God.' It must be said to the credit of those holding this opinion that they are jealous of the honor of the Lord and that they have seen that God is a most glorious and majestic being. God, they will argue, is the Almighty One, who sits in infinite splendor and unapproachable glory on the very throne of the universe. There is nothing beyond his power, and all things are under his control; all creation does his bidding. Now for this awesome being to be pictured as pleading with sinners through his servants, calling on men to come to him and beseeching them to receive pardon is abhorrent, they say. It lowers God to an unacceptable level and dishonors his holy name.

By adopting this attitude, its proponents are forced to insist that those passages of Scripture which speak of God as pleading and beseeching men must be understood in a quite different way than one would normally assume from a simple reading of them. They are forced, in my opinion, to a terrible abuse of the Word of God. The fact is that God is revealed in Scripture as being a God who does plead with men through his servants; he does call upon them to come to him and beseeches them to be reconciled: "...as I live, saith the Lord God, I have no pleasure in the death of the wicked; but that the wicked turn from his way and live: turn ye, turn ye from your evil ways; for why will ye die, O house of Israel?" (Ezek. 33:11); "Now then we are ambassadors for Christ, as though God did beseech you by us: we pray you in Christ's stead, be ye reconciled to God" (2 Cor. 5:20); "Ho, everyone that thirsteth, come ye to the waters, and he that hath no money; come ye, buy, and eat ... Incline your ear, and come unto me: hear, and your soul shall live" (Isa. 55:1-3).

Taking the above verses as being literally addressed to lost sinners need not be considered as being detrimental to God's glory, as 'lowering' him in any way, but ought to be the cause of provoking a spirit of adoring wonder in man, that such a God, who is indeed as glorious as has been acclaimed, nevertheless does condescend to call upon men, and to invite them to come to him in such a tender way. The majesty and holiness of God does not suffer embarrassment from such calls, but provides the backdrop against which the grace, mercy, love and infinite condescension of God is the more vividly seen. Our conclusions, as to what God is like, must be derived out of Scripture, rather than be imposed upon Scripture.

A further reason why the legitimacy of inviting sinners to Christ is questioned, lies in the claim that *"carnal men ought not to be exhorted to spiritual duties."* Repentance and faith, it is said, are spiritual duties, and therefore the unconverted ought not to be exhorted to exercise them. "No man can come to me, except the Father which hath sent me draw him" (John 6:44a); "Because the carnal mind is enmity against God: for it is not subject to the law of God, neither indeed can be. So then they that are in the flesh cannot please God" (Rom. 8:7-8); "But the natural man receiveth not the things of the Spirit of God for they are foolishness unto him: neither can he know them, because they are spiritually discerned" (1 Cor. 2:14). The clear facts indicated in these verses, it is claimed, indicate the folly of inviting and directing sinners to come to Christ. It ought not to be done. But is this so? Again, we begin by insisting that unconverted people were invited to come to Christ, and were directed to embrace the Savior in the Scriptures. It must also be noted that such invitations and directions were not only addressed to 'awakened' and 'conscious' sinners, but also to those who were quite the opposite. For instance, in Psalm 2 those urged to "kiss the Son" are the "kings of the earth" who are in defiant revolt against the Lord and his anointed (cf. vs.10, 12); and this "kissing of the Son" is clearly synonymous with "trusting in him" (v.12). In Psalm 4 those who "loved vanity and sought after lying" (v.2) are directed to "offer the sacrifice of righteousness and put your trust in the Lord" (v.5). In Acts 8 Simon Magus is directed by Peter to "repent and pray to God" (v.22), even though Peter had concluded that he was "in the gall of bitterness and in the bond of iniquity," and that "his heart was not right in the sight of God" (vs.21, 23). In Isaiah 55 it is the "wicked and unrighteous man" who is invited to seek the Lord and to call upon him (v.7). A simple reading of Scripture will demonstrate the fact that unconverted people, that is, dead, senseless sinners, were invited and directed to come to Christ. It is a tragic thing to see attempts being made to evacuate such scriptures of their evident significance merely to either adhere to a preconceived notion or force the verses to be 'consistent' with our theological system.

Furthermore the inability of a sinner to perform spiritual duties must not be thought to cancel out the need for him to be urged to do so for two other important reasons. First, that it is through the invitation to repent and believe that God quickens his elect into doing that very thing. It 'made no sense' for Ezekiel to command a heap of dry bones to live! Yet with the command there went out the power to do the thing commanded. It 'made no sense' for Jesus to command a dead man to come forth, but again, the command carried with it the power to do what was otherwise impossible to do. It must be admitted by all who treat the Bible seriously, that, since the Fall, men have been in a state of spiritual inability; in and of themselves they have not the power to come to Christ. God has, however, purposed to save a great, elect company out of mankind, and in saving them, intends to bring them to faith in Christ. The elect are not known to the preachers of the gospel, and the work of drawing them to Christ is God's work, not the preacher's. But God works through his servants and through the gospel message; and though those invited to come to Christ be in a state of spiritual inability, yet in the case of the elect, when God's time has come, the power to comply with the command and with the gospel terms will be transmitted to the sinner through the very gospel invitation. The dead shall live, the blind shall see, the deaf shall hear.

Again it needs to be stressed that the inability of the sinner is a sinful inability for which he is to be held responsible and guilty. It needs to be stressed that the inability of the sinner lies fundamentally in his sinful aversion to that which is holy and good. He loves darkness rather than light; his own inclinations are to the world and the flesh; he is a rebel who prefers his own way to God's way. His inability is not something which he can hide behind to excuse his unbelief, but a sinful inability comprised of a positive dislike of holiness and God's way which needs to be repented of. It is therefore important that he should be exhorted to repent and believe. His duty to do so must be pointed out so that he might be convinced of the sinfulness of his impenitent and unbelieving condition. Such invitations and directions also bring into focus his sinful disobedience and rebellion and demonstrate the justice of the judgment of God being visited upon him.

The third reason why some object to the inviting of sinners to Christ lies in the fact that they believe it to be 'a denial of the sovereignty of God.' Great emphasis is placed upon the fact that salvation is a work of God and that it is a work of his sovereign grace. He saves whom he will and when he will. To invite men to come to Christ, it is suggested, implies that man has some ability to come on his own, and that salvation is not a matter of sovereign grace. However, this is far from the truth. Inviting sinners to Christ does not teach the ability of the sinner, but the duty of the sinner; it also acknowledges the fact that according to God's own arrangement, those sinners who do come to Christ in repentance and faith shall be saved. Leaving all other questions aside for the moment, it must be acknowledged by all that those who come to Christ will be saved. It is therefore right that sinners should be invited to come. If it is their duty to do so, and if such incalculable blessings will accompany their doing so, every sinner ought to be invited and directed to come to Christ. The good pleasure of God's sovereign will which determines which sinners shall infallibly be brought to Christ is a matter of God's concern, not ours.

Again, the inviting of sinners to Christ does not deny the truth of God's sovereignty in the salvation of souls, but merely recognizes that the sovereign God has decreed the use of certain means to bring about certain ends. To cultivate the ground, sow the seed and fertilize the soil in no way implies that a farmer does not believe that the harvest depends on the sovereign pleasure of God! To say that God sovereignly saves whom he will, when he will, and that salvation is a work of sovereign grace is gloriously true and ought to be declared, but it is not the whole truth. It is also true that God is pleased, as we have said, to use means in accomplishing that end; and the means that he supremely uses is the preaching of the gospel accompanied by urgent and loving invitations to sinners to embrace the gospel and to come to Jesus Christ.

The various aspects of salvation are nowhere expressed more delightfully that in 2 Thess. 2:13-14. "But we are bound to give thanks always to God for you, brethren beloved of the Lord, because God hath from the beginning chosen you to salvation." Here is a clear declaration that the origin of the salvation of these sinners must be traced back to the fountain of divine election; God chose them to salvation. But the verse goes on, "God... hath chosen you to salvation, through sanctification of the Spirit and belief of the truth, whereunto he called you by our gospel to the obtaining of the glory of our Lord Jesus Christ." The fountainhead, the root cause, of their salvation having been declared to be the choice of God, the means in bringing that choice to actual fruition are then referred to. The purpose and the means to accomplish it are beautifully laid side by side.

B. The Confusion of Some Who Recognize the Truth of Sovereign Grace

There are some brethren who would not dream of trying to explain away the Scriptures which indicate the 'rightness' of inviting men to Christ. They recognize that our Lord and the apostles did so and they feel that they ought also to do so.

But there are those who are troubled, almost haunted, by this question: *"Is God really sincere in his invitation to sinners, can he be sincere in offering mercy to those whom he knows will not receive it when he knows that he has not purposed to extend that special grace to them which alone can reverse their unwillingness? Can the preacher, knowing that there are some whom God has determined to pass by, 'sincerely offer salvation to all, and in all sincerity call men to come to Christ?'"* This is a question which has hampered many good men in their gospel preaching. I believe that it is important for the preacher (or for the witnessing Christian for that matter) to be convinced in his own mind of the sincerity of God in his invitation to sinners. If the preacher is not convinced of this in his own mind, he will be hampered in his approach to the unconverted and troubled in conscience by his own ministry.

Is God sincere when he says, "I have no pleasure in the death of the wicked, but rather that he should turn and live"? Is he sincere when he says, "O that there were such an heart in them, that they would fear me, and keep all my commandments always, that it might be well with them, and with their children forever" (Deut. 5:29), and "Oh that my people had hearkened unto me, and Israel had walked in my ways" (Psa. 81:13), or is he playing some cynical game? How can he be sincere when, while uttering these statements, he withholds the power which could have effected the turning, the lack of which he laments? This is a profound and difficult question. It is discussed most helpfully by Robert Dabney, who points out that a person in a position of importance, involving many responsibilities, may sincerely desire a certain outcome of events, have the power to assure that outcome, and yet be restrained from exerting that power, because of other higher motives and considerations which may not be understood by others. He gives the example of General Washington signing the death warrant of Major Andre:

> In this historical instance we have these facts: Washington had plenary power to kill or save alive. His compassion for the criminal was real and profound. Yet he signed his death warrant with spontaneous decision. Washington's volition to sign the death warrant of Andre did not arise from the fact that his compassion was slight or feigned, but from the fact that it was rationally counterpoised by a complex of superior judgments and propensions [moral directions] of wisdom, duty, patriotism and moral indignation. Let us suppose that one of Andre's intercessors (and he had them, even among the Americans standing by) hearing the commanding general say, as he took up the pen to sign the fatal paper, "I do this with the deepest reluctance and pity," should have retorted, "since you are supreme in this matter, and have full bodily ability to throw down that pen, we shall know by your signing this warrant that your pity is hypocritical." The petulance of this charge would have been equal to its folly. The pity was real, but was restrained by superior element of motive. Washington had official and bodily power to discharge the criminal, but he had not the sanction of his own wisdom and justice. Thus the pity was genuine, and yet his volition not to indulge it was free and sovereign. [Robert L. Dabney, *Discussions Evangelical and Theological* (First published 1890, Reprint: London: Banner of Truth Trust, 1966), pp. 285-286].

Dabney has clearly put his finger on a crucial consideration. When God declares his compassion for sinners and his desire to see them turn and live, we are not to arrogantly assert, "If that were true then he would do something about it for he has the power." We are to recognize that there are a million considerations in the administration of this vast universe of which we know nothing at all, and if God does not put forth the power to overcome the sinful disobedience of some of his creatures there must be higher reasons which cause him not to do so, which do not in any way detract from his sincerity either in desiring the sinner to turn from his evil ways, or from his calling the sinner to do so. The expression of grief from God over the waywardness of his creatures; the earnest invitation and calls to them to repent of their sin and believe on the Saviour are not empty words, cruel teasing, as a cat playing with a mouse, before delivering the final blow. These are sincere words in which God means what he says. They are words which will be proved to be absolutely true and reliable by every sinner who responds to them. No preacher need feel restricted or bound by doubts of God's sincerity, he may follow his Lord in inviting sinners everywhere to "look and live."

Even when we are convinced of the sincerity of the call, some still have problems, especially in the area of Particular Redemption. "How," they ask, "can we invite all men to come to Christ when we are not sure that Christ has died for them, for particular redemption teaches that Christ died only for his elect?" I think that the heart of the answer to this problem lies in our grasping two things. First, that the 'limit' on the atonement is not related to its power or sufficiency, but to its intent and design. The sufferings of Christ would not have been increased if the number of the elect had been more than it actually is.

The value of Christ's sufferings cannot be calculated in such terms. The value of Christ's atonement is infinite by virtue of the infinite value of his person. The atonement of

Christ has no "limit" on it as far as its power and sufficiency is concerned. If every sinner in the world plus those of ten thousand other worlds should cast themselves on it for mercy it would not be overtaxed. The preacher should not be restricted in his gospel invitations by the thought, "but maybe Christ did not die for this one." Such a way of thinking ought not to be entertained for a moment. Rather let him be convinced that "sinners plunged beneath that flood lose all their guilty stains," and let him carry that good news to the sinners with whom he is speaking. The preacher does not need to concern himself with the question, "For whom did Christ die?" any more than he is to concern himself with the question, "Who are the elect?" This is the question for the preacher: "Can I tell any and every sinner that if he comes to God through Jesus Christ, and casts himself on the atonement of Jesus for the cleansing of his sins, he shall be pardoned?" The answer is an unequivocal YES!

II. Inviting Sinners to Christ is to be Safeguarded Against Distortions and Abuses

A. An Invitation to Come to Christ is not to be Confused with the Altar Call

Whilst the necessity of inviting sinners to Jesus is something to be defended, that invitation must be safeguarded. In the evangelism of today, inviting sinners to Christ, which is a matter related to preaching, has been confused with giving altar calls, which is something related to methodology. When today's preachers speak of "giving the invitation," they invariably mean giving an altar call in which people are bidden to walk to the front of the church or auditorium as an indication that they are 'accepting Christ.'

The great objection to this methodology is that it identifies a physical act with saving faith. No matter how carefully the preacher tries to explain that "coming to the front won't save you," the person being addressed can hardly be blamed for equating the two. All through the sermon he has been told of the importance of coming to Christ, and then at the end of the sermon he is exhorted, "Come to Jesus Christ right now; let this be the moment of decision; come as you are; he will receive you," and at the same time he is directed to come down to the front of the auditorium. I say he can hardly be blamed for believing in his own mind that coming down to the front was indeed that very 'coming to Jesus' of which the preacher had been so earnestly speaking.

There are many people whose lives give sad evidence that they are unregenerate, yet feel sure that they have been saved simply because they 'came to Jesus' by responding to an altar call. But coming to Christ is a purely spiritual matter. It has nothing to do with the movement of the hands or feet. Coming to Christ involves a response of the mind, heart, and will of the sinner (produced of course by the operation of the Spirit), but it is a dangerous thing to link this so closely to any form of altar call.

Many Christians are not aware of the fact that the altar call system, deemed by many today to be so essential to evangelism, was not known in Christian churches until the 19th century. It was Charles Finney who introduced and popularized the system (though occasionally similar methods had been used by some Methodists before Finney), and though it is perhaps consistent with Finney's theological views, it is hardly consistent with a Reformed and biblical doctrinal position. Men were invited to Christ, and by God's grace, came to Christ for 1,800 years before altar calls came to be used in churches. As sinners are invited to Christ through preaching, as Christ is declared and his gracious Gospel promises unfolded, and sinners are invited to 'look and live,' the Spirit of God will ensure that his Word shall not return unto him void.

B. The Appeal is to be Made to the Whole Man

In preaching the gospel and inviting sinners to come to Christ we must be sure to address the whole man. The weakness of much of today's evangelical preaching lies in the fact that often only an emotional response is sought. An assault on the emotions is made: moving illustrations, and heart-rending anecdotes or personal experiences are used. Soft music and even, at times, special lighting effects are used to produce an emotional response. The outlet for that response is often the altar call discussed above which is identified with coming to Christ. However, when the person is removed from that atmosphere, and returns to the cold world of reality, his 'decision' often proves to be spurious.

The inviting of sinners to Christ must be linked with an appeal to the whole person. There is no question that his emotions will be involved. How can one be unemotional when considering the cross and issues relating to the eternal welfare of the soul? The heart must be weaned from sin and the sinner must be brought to see Jesus as more desirable than all else. Only the Holy Spirit can do this of course, but the preacher will want to preach in such a way that the spirit will use his message in achieving these objectives. The way to the heart must be through the mind. Truth must be presented to the mind if the response of the heart is going to be a valid one. The great facts of the gospel must be presented. The sinner must understand the issues involved. The great truths of ruin, redemption and regeneration must be set before him; repentance and faith must be explained. The mind must be reached if the heart is to be rightly moved.

Of course, the mind being enlightened and the heart moved, the will must be exercised. The gospel is not merely a subject for examination, analysis or discussion, but for obedient response. Reformed preachers must not overreact to the false teaching of the day regarding 'free-will' by failing to recognize the true importance of the will in the conversion experience. As Moses deliberately chose to align himself with the afflicted people of God, and to reject the pleasures of Egypt, so men and women today must choose to walk in the ways of the Lord and reject the world. Reformed preachers ought to feel no hesitation in preaching, "Choose ye this day who ye will serve." Such preachers, will want their hearers to understand that the right choice of the will is to be attributed to the grace of the Spirit of God, not to themselves, but they ought still to press on the conscience of their hearers the necessity of the will responding obediently to the gospel.

C. Invite Men to the Biblical Jesus

This leads also to the importance of inviting men to the biblical Jesus. Again, the abuses of modem evangelism make it necessary to consider this need. The Christ which some have heard about is a revolutionary hero who can yet lead mankind into a social-economic utopia. He is a kind of first century Che Guevara, ready to lead the young rebels against the modem day establishment. The Christ that others have heard about is a psychiatrist-like figure who can take care of all their hang-ups, deliver them from all of their frustrations and cares and give them a life free from any difficulties and worries. He is one who, in a mysterious way, makes marriages full of grace and romance, businessmen eminently successful, and athletes game-winning heroes. Others have heard of a Jesus who can assure them a place in heaven, while allowing them to pursue a life of carnality down here. This Jesus lets you have the best of both worlds: he is a Savoir without being a Lord; he delivers without making demands.

In inviting sinners to Jesus we must make sure that we are inviting them to a biblical Jesus. I know of no better way to guard against a misleading view of Jesus than to think of him in terms of his threefold office of prophet, priest and king, and to proclaim him to men in this manner. This is not to say, of course, that it is not legitimate to single out one aspect of the person or work of Christ in preaching, but it is to say that men must be given to understand who it is they must receive in order to become the sons of God. We are to invite men to him as prophet; that is, one who will teach them the will of God, and one whose instruction they must believe and receive. We invite them to one who is priest; that is, one who offers up the atoning sacrifice for their sins, in whom alone they must rest to be cleansed from their sins. We invite them to one who is king; that is, one who will exercise rule over them, and to whom they owe allegiance.

If Christ is preached in his offices, and sinners recognize that it is to him that they are invited and must come, then much confusion and danger will be avoided. The current debate going on as to whether Christ must be received as

Lord as well as Savoir if a man is to be saved, must surely be settled if it be recognized that Christ must be preached in all of his offices. To say that Christ does not need to be received as Lord is to say that one may receive him as prophet and priest but not as king. Such an idea is preposterous. You cannot divide up Christ. He is what he is: prophet, priest and king. To receive him at all is to receive him as he is, in his three-fold office.

So in inviting sinners to Christ there are safeguards to be maintained. We must not confuse the invitation to come to Jesus with the altar call; we must address the whole man and we must invite him to a biblical Jesus.

III. Inviting Sinners to Christ is Necessary for the Health of the Church

A. The Importance of Concern for Souls

One of the dangers facing every church is that of becoming too inward looking: being too taken up with oneself and being careless and uninterested about the needs of others, particularly the lost. The incident recorded in 2 Kings 7 is a fascinating story with a powerful application. Here were four men so delighted with the good things they had discovered that they sat indulging themselves while a whole city was perishing nearby. They spoke accurately when they said, "...We do not well: this day is a day of good tidings and we hold our peace..." (2 Kings 7:9). How often has this been sadly true of whole congregations of Christians? They have fed their souls on the good things of God week after week and become so self-centered and inward in their thinking that they are never moved by the condition of the unsaved.

We must confess with shame, that some, having come to understand the doctrine of election and God's sovereignty in the application of redemption have become cold and insensitive to the condition of the lost. In this state they are a far cry from the Calvinistic worthies they claim to admire. Who can read the words of Spurgeon, Baxter, Brainerd or Whitefield without feeling the throb of compassion for souls? Who can read of the Lord himself weeping over the city of Jerusalem, or comparing the multitudes to sheep without a shepherd, and not realize that our Lord himself knew the reality of concern for the lost? It is a drastic revelation when commentators seek to rob such passages of their obvious significance in order to deny our Lord the feeling which they themselves do not possess. The Calvinism of the Bible (if I might be allowed to use such an expression) is a Calvinism suffused with concern for the souls of men and if the revived Calvinism of our day is to be worth maintaining it must be that kind of Calvinism. We must be concerned for the salvation of sinners; we need a spirit that longs to see the multitudes gathered into the kingdom of God.

Now I realize that the mere inviting of sinners to come to Christ will not produce such a concern of itself; many factors will be involved in producing that. But I dare to suggest that where a pastor does not engage in inviting sinners to Jesus; where the preaching consistently lacks in the calls and invitations of the gospel, then it will be extremely difficult to maintain and nurture concern for souls in the hearts of people. The very exposition of the gracious gospel promises and their earnest application to the hearts of sinners will do much to stir up concern for the lost in the hearts of God's people.

B. Presenting a Truly Biblical View of God

To do justice to God's being and character in our preaching is a demanding task, and the character of God is another area where modern preaching has often been sadly lacking. God has been presented as a well-meaning old gentleman, earnestly desiring to do good and bless men, but constantly being foiled in his attempt by his rebellious creatures. The picture of Jesus most familiar to evangelicals today is the one where he stands forlornly at the barred door of man's heart, seeking entrance, but powerless to do anything about the discouraging situation. God is so often presented as one to be sympathized with or even pitied, rather than worshipped. So here, as in other areas, it is possible for Reformed preachers to overreact.

Revolting against this caricature of God, they may be inclined to so stress his might, power and awesome majesty and the fact that he saves whom he will, that their listeners may get the impression that God really isn't the least bit concerned about lost sinners. The answer to an extreme presentation of God on one side is not to present just as extreme a view on the other side! The antidote surely is to try and present a balanced view, to try to display all aspects of his divine character; to acknowledge, as Paul did, that in God one may behold "goodness and severity" (Rom. 11:22). We will not be helping the Reformed cause if we give to our hearers the impression that God could not care less about the condition of the lost, nor will we be true to the Word of God.

That most beautiful of all parables, the Prodigal Son, was given to counteract that very idea. How graphically did the Lord Jesus teach us that God delighted to receive the returning prodigal. Did not that Father who ran out to meet his son, who fell on his neck and kissed him, have a concerned heart when he was in the far country? Was he not moved with compassion for that boy? One of the ways in which we will present a balanced view of God to our people is by unfailingly declaring the invitation of the gospel to sinners. In those invitations our people will recognize the voice of a God of compassion and mercy; a God of grace and love; a God of pity and tender mercy. They will rejoice in his holiness, justice and truth, of which they will hear, but the publication of the invitation of the gospel will help them maintain a biblical view of God, not an unbalanced one.

The invitations of the gospel to sinners ought to be urgent and warmhearted. We must prayerfully seek for the compassion and sincerity of Christ. It is not a question of simply doing that which is orthodox, and therefore, if inviting sinners to Christ is orthodox then we had better do it. Our preaching needs to be of the kind that seeks to "compel them to come in." It is recorded of a particular Puritan preacher that he 'melted over his congregation.' His preaching seemed to be embracing his people in arms of love, and constraining them by tenderness to come to the fold of Christ. Such preaching we need today. Let us not be inhibited in inviting sinners to Jesus, and may God be pleased to bless the invitations to the salvation of multitudes.

Bibliography for Part One:

Dabney, Robert. "God's Indiscriminate Proposals of Mercy as Related to His Power, Wisdom and Sincerity." In *Discussions Evangelical and Theological, Vol. 1*. London: The Banner of Truth Trust, 1967.

Fuller, Andrew. *The Gospel Worthy of All Acceptation*. H&E Phinney, 1809.

Hulse, Erroll. *The Free Offer of the Gospel*. Haywards Heath, England: Carey Publications, 1973.

M'Lean, Archibald. *The Calls and Invitations of the Gospel*. Edinburgh, 1823.

The Banner of Truth, Vol.1, issues 1-16; Vol. 2, issues 52-75. London: 1961 & 1967.

PART TWO: LIMITED ATONEMENT
ITS IMPLICATIONS FOR EVANGELISM

It should be made clear at the outset that no attempt is being made here to prove or defend the doctrine of limited atonement. I begin by assuming that this doctrine is accepted as being biblical and therefore true by those who are reading this booklet; or at least that the reasons for upholding the position known as limited atonement are known and understood. Furthermore, it is not our purpose in this paper to discuss the merit or demerit of the expression limited atonement. The expressions *particular redemption* or *definite atonement* are probably preferred by most reading this paper, and indeed they are preferred by the author of the paper, but *limited atonement* has probably had a wider usage than these other two.

A. The Implications with Respect to Motivation.

It is a great encouragement for evangelism. It might be considered a strange thing by some people in the world of religion to suggest that the doctrine of limited atonement can in any way be said to be an encouragement to evangelism. One of the reasons why such people are so strongly opposed to the doctrine is because they consider that it must be a mortal enemy of evangelistic endeavor. However, it is an encouragement in a very real way.

One of the reasons why the expression *definite atonement* is often preferred to *limited atonement* is because the doctrine is seeking to emphasize the fact that Christ's atonement as presented in the Bible did indeed accomplish that which it was intended to accomplish. Proponents of this doctrine rightly emphasize that the atonement of the Bible is not an atonement which merely makes men redeemable but one which actually redeemed those for whom it was offered. The shedding of Christ's blood did not merely make men savable but it actually and definitely saved those for whom it was shed. The atonement infallibly secured the salvation of all those for whom it was offered. This *definite* character of the atonement is brought out in verses such as Rom. 5:10: *we were reconciled to God by the death of His Son;* Gal. 3:13: *Christ hath redeemed us from the curse of the law, being made a curse for us;* and Heb. 9:12: *by His own blood he entered in once into the Holy Place, having obtained eternal redemption for us.*

The element of substitution, which is the very heart of the gospel, declares that there is a people, known to God, and chosen by him, for whom Jesus Christ did stand as a surety. There are those for whose sins he has paid, and who by the very justice of God must be delivered from the guilt and bondage of sin. This truth of limited atonement, therefore, like the other aspects of truth which we refer to as the doctrines of grace, carries with it a note of certainty and confidence with respect to the conversion of sinners.

The redemption which has been planned by the Father and executed by the Son MUST be applied by the Spirit. Therefore the person who believes in limited atonement, believes in an atonement which has been efficacious, and which is part of a divine purpose which must result in the conversion of sinners. He is therefore encouraged to evangelize by the fact that he is not engaged in an uncertain enterprise with no real assurance of success, but he is encouraged to believe that evangelistic labors will succeed just because they are founded on an atonement which has already succeeded.

This grand element of certainty, and its clear relationship to Christ's atonement is seen in the tenth chapter of John's gospel where we have the important teaching of Christ as the Good Shepherd who lays down his life for the sheep. In the sixteenth verse of the chapter, the Lord Jesus says *and other sheep I have, which are not of this fold: them also I MUST bring; and they SHALL hear my voice....* The vision which John received in the seventh chapter of Revelation reveals that the purchase of Christ's blood includes people of every kindred, tribe and nation, and is again an encouragement for an evangelism which is extensive, indeed worldwide, and sure of the blessing of God.

It assures that the sufficiency of the message is preached. A grasp of the truth of limited atonement enables the one evangelizing to feel that he has a complete gospel to proclaim, and an all-sufficient savior to set before sinners. The difference between the concepts of universal atonement and limited atonement has been expressed in popular form by comparing them to bridges spanning a chasm. Universal atonement is like a bridge which stretches right along the length of the chasm; it is broad indeed, but the problem with it is that it doesn't take a person completely over to the other side; it stops half-way. Limited atonement, on the other hand, is narrower, but it goes right across to the other side.

The proponents of universal atonement must proclaim an atonement which leaves men short of being redeemed, and which, when all is said and done, is dependent on something in the sinner to make it efficacious. The proponent of limited atonement on the other hand, while recognizing the

necessity of the sinner's repentance and faith is able to proclaim an atonement which has purchased the very grace
which produces those blessed effects in the sinner's heart.
He can tell the sinner who feels the hardness of his heart,
and the terrible absence of those things which God demands
from him, to look to a Christ who has purchased them all
and who is able to give him all that he needs, seeing that he
purchased them with his precious blood. Joseph Hart ex-
presses it beautifully in a lovely hymn:

> Come ye needy, come and welcome
> God's free bounty glorify;
> True belief and true repentance,
> every grace that brings you nigh,
> without money, Come to Jesus Christ and buy.

Limited atonement, rather than impoverishing the gospel,
enhances it, and gives a man to feel that he has a great message to present to men; and this of course acts as a motivation, that he should seek to communicate this great gospel to
others.

*The effect of the doctrine on the Christian witnessing or the
evangelist preaching.* This might be considered a very subjec-
tive thing but I believe it is very relevant. In 2 Cor. 5:14 Paul
speaks about the love of Christ constraining him. The apos-
tle meant, not his own love for Christ, but his apprehension
of Christ's love for him. The more he grasped and understood of Christ's love toward himself, the more constrained
he was to serve him and glorify his name. This presents an
important principle to us; that the mainspring of Christian
service (indeed it should be the mainspring of the entire
Christian life) is love toward the Savior. When a sinner
grasps the love that Christ has had toward him, that sinner

will gladly suffer for Jesus, and live out his life in his service. But what more stunning message of the love of Christ to us is there than the message of a *particular redemption?* To know that Jesus Christ died for ME; that his atonement was not just a vague general 'something' done for everyone in general but none in particular, but that I was on his heart when he died; that is a shattering revelation; that brings the soul down low before the cross in wonder and in awe.

This is the sense of amazement which comes through in the words of Paul in Gal 2:20: *the Son of God who loved me and gave himself for me.* Now I suggest that when a person has been gripped with that truth, it will be his desire to tell of this glorious Savior to all he possibly can. This truth will fire the heart, and produce a great desire to glorify the Savoir, and knowing that the Savoir is glorified by obedience he will seek to obey him in the work of evangelism; and knowing that the Savoir is glorified when souls come to him and acknowledge him as Savoir and Lord, he cannot then fail to have a strong desire to see them come.

So much then for the implications of this doctrine in the area of motivation. Let us now consider:

B. Implications with Respect to the Substance of Evangelistic Preaching.

Some time ago I was speaking to a lady on the question of the salvation of the soul, and she said words to this effect: "I now understand that in order to be saved, I must not just believe that Christ died for sinners, but that he died for ME." She was echoing what has become common in evangelical Christianity: the idea that the essence of being saved was to believe that Christ died for me. If I can be persuaded that is true, and be persuaded to acknowledge and testify to it, I am saved. However this is not only not true, but it is also potentially dangerous to the soul. For a person might be persuaded that Christ died for him, and yet never actually be brought to the place of exercising hearty and penitent faith in the Lord Jesus Christ. The Bible does not call upon men to believe that Christ died for them in order that they might be saved, but rather to repent of their sin and to trust in the Lord Jesus, resting in the efficacy of his atoning blood to cleanse them from their sins. The two things are quite different.

If the doctrine of universal atonement is true, which would probably be claimed by those using the approach referred to above, then it is simply a matter of fact that Christ died for every single individual in the world without exception. It would be entirely possible therefore to persuade a person to believe that 'truth,' and therefore have them to acknowledge "Yes, I believe that Christ died for ME," and yet for that to be a purely intellectual assent devoid of saving faith. He might be persuaded to believe that 'truth' in just the same way that he might be persuaded to believe that the Bible taught that God exists in a Trinity of persons. The doctrine of limited atonement makes it apparent that a person cannot know whether Christ died for HIM or not, until he has actually come to Christ in repentance and faith.

In evangelistic preaching therefore, it is not for the evangelist to tell unbelieving sinners (whether it be one or a thousand) that they must believe that Christ died for them, for that is something which neither the evangelist nor his audience can infallibly know. What he can tell them, and ought to tell them, is that Christ's atonement is gloriously sufficient to blot out the sins of any and every sinner who comes to him in repentance and faith; that God has promised that every coming one shall be cleansed in that precious blood and that therefore their great need and immediate duty is that they should come in repentance and faith to the Savoir who has promised to receive and save everyone without exception who does so come. Knowing that Christ died for ME is in fact a matter relating to assurance rather than being saved. Let us listen to Spurgeon on this subject in an excerpt taken from one of his sermons:

> I have sometimes thought when I have heard addresses from some revival brethren who kept on saying "believe, believe, believe," that I should like to have known for myself what it were to believe in order to our salvation. There is I fear a great deal of vagueness and crudeness about this matter. I have heard it often asserted that if you believe that Jesus Christ died for you then you will be saved. My dear hearer, do not be deluded by such an idea. You may believe that Jesus Christ died for you, and may believe what is not true; you may believe that which will bring you no sort of good whatsoever. That is not saving faith. The man who has saving faith afterward attains to the conviction that Christ died for him, but it is not of the essence of saving faith. Do not get that into your head or it will ruin you. Do not say, "I believe that Jesus Christ died for me," and because of that feel you are saved. I pray you to remember that the genuine faith that saves the soul has for its main element *trust*, absolute rest of the whole soul on the Lord Jesus Christ to save me, whether he died in particular or in special to save me or not, and relying, as I am, wholly and alone on him, I am saved. Afterward I come to perceive that I have a special interest in the Savior's blood; but if I think I have perceived that before I have believed in Christ, then I have inverted the Scriptural order of things, and I have taken as a fruit

of my faith that which is only to be obtained by rights, by the man who absolutely trusts in Christ and Christ alone to save.

In evangelism then, whether corporate or personal, the evangelist is not called upon to tell people that Christ died for them, and that they must believe that in order to be saved; but he is to tell them that the blood of Jesus Christ is sufficient to purge the sins of everyone who will trust him; and that they must trust themselves to him, the crucified and risen Lord, and to no one else, in order that they might be saved.

In order that we might underline the relevance of our grasping this aspect of things let me quote the testimony of a modern-day English Baptist minister who was having difficulty grappling with the question of how he could make a 'free' or indiscriminate offer of the gospel while he believed in a limited atonement. The minister said:

> This seemed inconsistent with limited atonement because it seemed to suppose that the God of Truth was asking hypothetically non-elect men and women to believe that Christ died for them—for whom he did not die. I later found the solution to this when the Puritans reminded me that justifying faith in relation to the atonement does not consist in believing that Christ died for ME (which is assurance), but in believing that salvation is only found through his work on the cross and in applying for an interest and share in it.

While we certainly would not desire to see those who believe in limited atonement become slaves to words and phrases, and getting into bondage over terminology, yet I believe that a knowledge of that truth will cause a man to be careful in what he says in the process of evangelism. Surely we are to be careful in proclaiming God's truth, and our words may have a very profound effect upon the one who listens to us. If the truth and the implications of limited atonement have come across to us we will be delivered from the tragic doubletalk which Arminian brethren are so often forced to use. A sad example of this appeared some years ago in a popular Sunday School publication, an adult 'take home' paper. The article was entitled "What Is Christianity," and in the midst of his presentation the author said:

> He voluntarily let men murder him in a bloody death. He said two things about that death. First, he was substituting for us humans in death row—that if we were willing to let him substitute (that is the righteous for the unrighteous) then in God's record book Christ's death would be substituted for ours.

Because the author insisted on universal redemption and yet wanted to hold on to the concept of substitution, he has effectively emptied the word substitution of all meaning, and become involved in a pathetic doubletalk. Either the Lord Jesus was our substitute those 2000 years ago or he was not. He cannot have actually been our substitute on the cross, and then only be our substitute 'if we will let him'! Such talk cheapens the atonement and empties great words of their true significance. Limited atonement must cause us to be careful that we do not misrepresent the gospel, and that we speak clearly and carefully what God has said.

Before we leave this point concerning the substance of preaching, let me make two further observations which come under the title of *implications*. First, I would emphasize that the fact that an evangelist has no real right to tell unbelievers "Christ died for you" does not deprive him of anything really worthwhile. There are many statements which can be made indiscriminately which are both arresting and scriptural. He may state that Christ died for sinners; Christ died for the ungodly; Christ died for the sins of his people; Christ died to take away sin, etc. It is also the preacher's privilege to expound the meaning of the cross, and to open up such tremendous words as *propitiation, reconciliation, surety, substitute, satisfaction, blood, died for,* etc.

The other observation is this, that our discussion in the area of the substance of preaching thus far, has surely brought to the surface the fact that when one holds to limited atonement one is not only not deprived of being able to preach to unconverted people about the cross, but that this doctrine will also cause the evangelist to emphasize and make much of the sinner's responsibility in repenting and believing. This I believe is essential, especially in our day when many unbiblical phrases are used in evangelistic preaching (make a decision for Christ; open your heart to Jesus; make a commitment to Christ; etc.) which may all be used and yet still leave a sinner ignorant of what repentance and faith really are, and the necessity of him exercising these graces.

C. Implications with Respect to the Universal Offer of the Gospel

As has been intimated already, there have been some who have had difficulty reconciling the doctrine of limited atonement with the duty and necessity of preaching the gospel to every creature, or with the "universal offer of the gospel," as it has sometimes been called. In seeking to provide a brief historical background it would be interesting to note that those who are considered by all to be 'standard reference' with respect to 'Calvinism,' and who would be charged (though quite erroneously) by some with being hyper-Calvinists not interested in evangelism, have nevertheless firmly maintained both limited atonement and the necessity of a universal offer of the gospel. For instance the participants in the Synod of Dort stated:

> It is the promise of the gospel that whosoever believeth in the gospel should not perish but have everlasting life: which promise, together with the injunction of repentance and faith, ought promiscuously, and without distinction, to be declared and published to all men and people.

Again the Westminster Confession of Faith declared:

> He freely offereth unto sinners life and salvation by Jesus Christ, requiring of them faith in him that they might be saved.

John Calvin wrote:

> The mercy of God is offered equally to those who believe and to those who believe not.

John Owen stated:

> The general publishing of the gospel unto "all nations" with the right that it hath to be preached to "every creature", Matt. 28:19; Mk. 16:15; because the way of salvation it declares is wide enough for all to walk in. There is enough in the remedy it brings to light to heal all their diseases, to deliver them from all their evils. If there were a thousand worlds, the gospel of Christ might, upon this ground, be preached to them all, if so be they will derive virtue from him by touching him in faith; the only way to draw refreshment from this fountain of salvation. It is then altogether in vain which some object, that the preaching of the gospel to all is altogether needless and useless if Christ died not for all, yea that it is to make God call upon men to believe that which is not true—namely that Christ died

for them; for first, beside that amongst those nations whither the gospel is sent there are some to be saved *(I have much people)* which they cannot be, in the way that God hath appointed to do it, unless the gospel be preached to others as well as themselves; and besides secondly, that in the economy and dispensation of the new covenant, by which all external differences and privileges of people, tongue and nations being abolished, and taken away, the word of grace was to be preached without distinction, and all men called everywhere to repent; and thirdly, that when God calleth upon men to believe, he doth not, in the first place call upon them to believe that Christ died for them, but that there is no name under heaven whereby they must be saved, but only of Jesus Christ, through whom salvation is preached; I say besides these certain truths, fully taking off that objection, this one thing of which we speak is a sufficient basis and ground for all those general precepts of preaching the gospel unto all men, even that sufficiency which we have described.

Many other witnesses might be summoned, but surely these words, coming as they do from those who were the leading proponents of limited atonement, indicate that this doctrine did not in any way cause them to withdraw from the necessity of the universal offer.

However the history of the church reveals that there were those in later years, who, departing from the position of these great men whom we have just quoted, did get to the place where they declared that the free offer of the Gospel to sinners indiscriminately was wrong. However it would be correct to say that the opposition of such men to the universal offer of the gospel was not so much based upon their understanding of limited atonement, but on their understanding of the doctrine of total depravity. However, be that as it may, there did arise amongst the ranks of Reformed bodies those who were opposed to the universal offer of the gospel, and Hyper-Calvinism did obtain a grip on many.

This fact may be seen from the famous Marrow controversy in the Church of Scotland in the early part of the 18th century. The controversy takes its name from a book called *The Marrow of Modern Divinity* which was written (or more correctly compiled) by a man named Edward Fisher. The book was a compilation of the "marrowy passages of the acknowledged masters of divinity," and set forth the scriptural balance between truths relating to sovereign grace and the universal offer of the gospel, as it was held by the Puritan worthies. The book was first published in 1646; a copy providentially came into the hands of the great Scottish preacher Thomas Boston in 1700, and a new edition was published in Scotland in 1718. The fact that Hyper-Calvinism had gripped much of the Church of Scotland at that point is attested to by the fact that the republishing of the *Marrow* caused a great stir, and that it was condemned by the general assembly of the Church of Scotland. Three great names in Church history are associated with the defense of the book and the position it espoused: Thomas Boston, Ralph Erskine and Ebenezer Erskine.

In his biographical introduction of Boston's great book *Human Nature in Its Fourfold State* Rev. George H. Morrison states:

> It would be an interesting, though by no means an easy task, to trace the influence of the Marrow, and of the Marrow controversy, upon religious Scotland. Weighted with the authority of saintly names, and rich in the added interest of church debate, the book was read by multitudes, and proved to

many "a light struck up in darkness." It was interpreted in some of Boston's most familiar writings. Men caught the echoes of it in the preaching of George Whitfield. It was a silent witness against the dry morality of countless pulpits. And if the nation was at all in readiness for the evangelical revival of the succeeding century, directly and indirectly the Marrow had played its part in that.

The problem of holding the balance between the Reformed faith, the doctrine of limited atonement being a part of that, and the universal offer was also seen in England. This may be seen in the history of Andrew Fuller, one of the great names forever identified with William Carey in the work of missions. Fuller, who was born in 1754, had been brought up under a ministry influenced by the type of preaching which did not believe in the universal offer. It was, as one expressed it "preaching of the Gill type." Fuller was called to the pastorate at the age of 21, and early in his ministry he received help from the writings of Bunyan and Gill. However he soon realized that there was a great difference between the two men. Whilst they both adhered firmly to Calvinistic theology, limited atonement included, Bunyan obviously felt no hesitancy in inviting all sinners everywhere to come to Christ, whereas Gill would never do such a thing. After much prayer and study Fuller came to the conclusion that Bunyan was scriptural in this, and that Gill was not. Fuller's convictions eventually led to his writing the famous book called *The Gospel Worthy of All Acceptation,* and it was a direct result of this book that Carey went with the gospel to India. T. E. Watson stated:

> It is no exaggeration to say that Carey's going to India was the logical outcome of Fuller's emancipation from hyper-Calvinism. Fuller maintained that the gospel was worthy of

ALL acceptation, from which Carey deduced that its acceptance ought to be pressed on ALL mankind.

Sad to say it is true today, at least in England, that there are those who would still deny the necessity and duty of extending the offer of the gospel to all men everywhere, but as we have sought to demonstrate this is in contrast to those who have been the greatest luminaries in the Christian church, and in the Reformed faith. We would add this note in leaving this brief historical sketch, that in departing from the hyper-Calvinistic position where there was no free offer of the gospel men such as Boston and Fuller did not become Arminians! Fuller for instance in a letter to Dr. Ryland said:

> If my present connection (the particular Baptists) were to disown me, I should rather choose to go through the world alone than be connected with them (the Arminian Baptists).

As Erroll Hulse said "he was well and truly fixed in the saddle of Puritan theology without any danger of falling off front, back, or sides."

We may clearly say that there is no inconsistency in a man holding to the doctrine of limited atonement and seeking in evangelism to bid all men receive mercy and pardon from God's hand. This is so first of all because the call of the evangelist summoning men to turn to Christ is not based (as we have before stated) on a knowledge that Christ died for them, anymore than it is based on the knowledge that the Father has elected them. The evangelist does not know who those are for whom Christ has died; but he does know that God has called on all men everywhere to repent, and to look to him. By the same token a man is not bidden to come to Christ because he knows that Christ has died for him, but he is bidden to come to Christ because God commands and invites him to do so, and there is salvation in none other but the Lord Jesus. Who those are for whom Christ has died is one of those secret things which belong unto the Lord our God; his invitations to all men everywhere to look to him are among those things revealed unto us and unto our children. The command and invitation of God to all men everywhere to repent and believe the gospel is seen in such verses as:

Now [God] *commandeth all men everywhere to repent.* Acts 17:30

Ho, everyone that thirsteth, come ye to the waters, and he that hath no money; come ye, buy, and eat; yea, come, buy wine and milk, without money and without price. Isa 55:1

Look unto me, and be ye saved, all the ends of the earth: for I am God and there is none else. Isa 45:22

All the warrant that a man needs to maintain a free offer of the gospel to all creatures is the command and promise of God. And all the warrant a sinner needs for coming to God through Jesus Christ is the same divine command and promise.

However we might also add that the grounds for the offer of salvation to all men rests not only on the command and promise of God, but on the fact of the sufficiency of the atonement to cleanse any and all who entrust themselves to it. The limit in the atonement is not in any way related to its power, and there never has been and never will be a sinner who ever sought sincerely to wash in the blood of the lamb who found that there was not cleansing there for him. Men are to be exhorted to come without delay and without fear to an atonement which is sufficient for everyone who comes; and those who come will truly be cleansed from sin.

I would like to close by giving two quotations from two outstanding servants of God of the past. Whilst the quotes are rather lengthy, they nevertheless express beautifully that which we are seeking to express in this last point, and they make an excellent conclusion to this booklet. The first is from the great work of John Owen *The Death of Death in the Death of Christ.*

We must exactly distinguish between man's duty and God's purpose, there being no connection between them. The purpose and decree of God is not the rule of our duty; neither is the performance of our duty in doing what we are commanded any declaration of what is God's purpose to do, or his decree that it should be done. Especially is this to be seen and considered in the duty of the ministers of the Gospel, in the dispensing of the word, in exhortations, invitations, precepts and threatenings, committed unto them; all of which are perpetual declaratives of our duty, and do manifest the approbation of the thing exhorted and invited to, with the truth of the connection between one thing and another, but not of the counsel and purpose of God, in respect of individual persons, in the ministry of the word. A minister is not to make enquiry after, nor to trouble himself about, those secrets of the eternal mind of God, namely—whom he purposeth to save, and whom he hath sent Christ to die for in particular. It is enough for them to search his revealed will, and thence take their directions, from whence they have their commission. Wherefore there is no sequel between the universal precepts from the word concerning the things, unto God's purpose in himself concerning the persons. They command and invite all to repent and believe; but they know not in particular on whom God will bestow repentance unto salvation, nor in whom he will effect the work of faith with power. And when they make proffers and tenders in the name of God to all, they do not say to all "it is the purpose and intention of God that ye should believe" (who gave them any such power), but that it is his command, which makes it their duty to do what is required of them; and they do not declare his mind, what himself in particular will do. The external offer is one from which every man may conclude his own duty; none, God's purpose which yet may be known upon performance of his duty. Their objection then is vain, who affirm that God hath given Christ for all to whom he offers Christ in the preaching of the gospel; for his offer in the preaching of the gospel is not declarative to any in particular, neither of what God hath done, nor of what he will do in reference to him, but of what he ought to do if he would be approved of God and obtain the good things promised. When it will follow:

First, that God always intends to save some among them to whom he sends the gospel in its power. And the ministers of it being first, unacquainted with his particular purpose; secondly, bound to seek the good of all and everyone, as much as in them lies; thirdly, to hope and judge well of all, even as it is meet for them—they may make a proffer of Jesus Christ, with life and salvation in him, notwithstanding that the Lord hath given his Son only to his elect.

Secondly, that this offer is neither vain nor fruitless, being declarative of their duty, and of what is acceptable to God if it be performed as it ought to be, even as it is required. And if any ask, what it is of the mind and will of God that is declared and made known when men are commanded to believe for whom Christ did not die? I answer first, what they ought to do, if they will do that which is acceptable with God; secondly, the sufficiency of salvation that is in Jesus Christ to all that believe on him; thirdly, the certain infallible, inviolable connection that is between faith and salvation, so that whosoever performs the one shall surely enjoy the other, for whoever comes to Christ he will in no wise cast out.

Our second and concluding quotation is from a sermon by John Bonar, the cousin of Andrew Bonar:

But still an objector may say, you offer what is not there; there is nothing in your system except an offer; there is nothing behind it; there is no reality. But where is it, we ask, that there is nothing? Is it in the original design and eternal purpose of God? And is there more in that original design and eternal purpose of God in any system but that of universal salvation? Or is it in the work of Christ that there is nothing? There is glorious sufficiency in it. The atonement is complete; nothing needs to be, nothing can be, added to it. His work is perfect— the righteousness is perfect—the intercession is all prevailing to the very uttermost. Or, finally is it in the offer that there is nothing? There is the most blessed certainty—the largest, the fullest extent in it—and what could there be more of in any offer?

But still proud man, after all, returns and asks, how can you sincerely offer what you say it may not be God's design actually to bestow? And, growing more bold, he says, how can God offer that to all which is not meant for all? This, instead of an offer of mercy is but a mocking, a deceiving of man. This is fearful language for a man to use, but there is no foundation for it. No! God neither mocks nor deceives anyone. Where there is no confidence placed, there can be no deceit experienced. Where there is confidence placed, there the blessing is received. There is no deceit, and from this God shall stand forever infinitely clear. No man surely would have God to fulfill his word of promise to those who do not believe it, and do not claim its fulfillment. And whoever believes it, and claims the fulfillment, to him shall it be made fully and gloriously good, and good forever.

Putting down then all such contendings against God, and escaping from the unwholesome atmosphere whence they spring, let us return to rejoice in the full warrant which every minister has to offer Christ to all—and the full warrant which each has to receive Christ for himself. Christ is set forth to us not only as a priest offering a sacrifice for sin, but as a prophet and a king; and as such is made known to us to be received and rested on. The benefits of justification, adoption and sanctification are freely offered in him. This offer is to be made to every creature under heaven on the authority of God. They only who refuse this offered grace perish in their sins; they who believe it and receive it, live and rejoice—joy in God through Jesus Christ, by whom they have received the atonement.

Thus without seeking to scan the unrevealed mysteries of the book of God's decree—without defacing the works of Christ—without blotting out the word of God and all that is said of God's sovereign grace and electing love—without destroying the object of faith, in order to make it acceptable to those who love not God—without reducing the blessed word to a few portions of it, and wishing to forget all the rest—without such things as these, there is a full and blessed warrant to come to each sinner, wherever he is, and say *unto you the voice of Christ comes, turn and live; look unto me and be ye saved.* It is the command of God to offer Christ—*Go ye and preach to all nations.* It is the command of God to receive him—*this is the work of God that ye should believe on him whom he hath sent.* It is the invitation of God to come to him; and it is the promise of God, that whosoever cometh shall in no wise be cast out. *The Spirit says come, and the bride saith come; and whosoever will, let him come and take of the water of life freely.*

Bibliography for Part Two

Boston, Thomas. *Human Nature in its Fourfold State.* London: The Banner of Truth Trust, 1964.

Cunningham, William. *Historical Theology, Vol. 2.* London: The Banner of Truth Trust. 1960.

Dabney, R. L. *Discussions Evangelical and Theological, Vol. 1.* London: The Banner of Truth Trust, 1967

Hulse, Erroll. *The Free Offer of the Gospel.* Haywards Heath, England: Carey Publications, 1973

Hulse, Erroll. *An Introduction to the Baptists.* Haywards Heath, England: Carey Publications, 1973

Owen, John. "The Death of Death in the Death of Christ." In *The Works of John Owen, Vol. 10.* London: The Banner of Truth Trust, 1965.

Packer, J. I. *Evangelism and the Sovereignty of God.* London: Inter-Varsity Fellowship, 1961.

Pink, A. W. *The Satisfaction of Christ.* Swengel, PA: Bible Truth Depot.

The Banner of Truth, articles in July 1958, Feb. 1959, Aug.-Oct. 1968, July-Aug. 1973.